PUFFIN B

HERE'S H

Hanson are no ordinary band. They are a p...
Isaac, Taylor and Zachary were just sixteen, fourteen and
eleven when they had their first smash hit with
'MMMbop'. Since then they've been top of the singles
and album charts in the UK, the USA and Australia
simultaneously – a feat no other band in history has
managed to achieve. These boys are here to stay.

Jeremy Case

Here's Hanson

PUFFIN BOOKS

PUFFIN BOOKS

Published by the Penguin Group
Penguin Books Ltd, 27 Wrights Lane, London w8 5tz, England
Penguin Putnam Inc., 375 Hudson Street, New York, New York 10014, USA
Penguin Books Australia Ltd, Ringwood, Victoria, Australia
Penguin Books Canada Ltd, 10 Alcorn Avenue, Toronto, Ontario, Canada m4v 3b2
Penguin Books (NZ) Ltd, 182–190 Wairau Road, Auckland 10, New Zealand

Penguin Books Ltd, Registered Offices: Harmondsworth, Middlesex, England

First published 1998
1 3 5 7 9 10 8 6 4 2

Text copyright © Jeremy Case, 1998
Photo insert copyright details:
Page i © Clemens Rikken/Sunshine, 1997
Page ii © David Atlas, 1997
Pages iii, iv, vii, viii © Ernie Paniccioli, 1997
Page v © Larry Busacca, 1997
Page vi © David Tonge, 1997
All pictures supplied by Retna.
All rights reserved

The moral right of the author and illustrator has been asserted

Set in Bembo
Made and printed in England by Clays Ltd, St Ives plc

British Library Cataloguing in Publication Data
A CIP catalogue record for this book is available from the British Library

ISBN 0–141–30227–5

Contents

CHAPTER ONE

Summer Lovin'

They should have named the album *Middle Of Everywhere*, because that's where Hanson have been ever since they blasted the cobwebs out of the charts with 'MMMBop', the single with the chorus that's catchier than the flu. Along with the jaunty melody, upbeat tempo and perfect harmonies, it was a ray of sunshine that defined the sound of summer. It forced a smile on to your lips and packed up all your troubles in an old kit bag. Destined to become an all-time pop classic, 'MMMBop' was such an instant smash that you could remember exactly where you were and what you were doing the first time you heard it.

The public loved it. And the three American brothers, whose combined age was less than many of the DJs who were playing their record, had a worldwide hit on their hands. 'MMMBop' went on to reach the number one slot in twenty countries, selling over four million copies world-wide. Hanson became the only band ever to have had a number one hit with their first single in both America and the UK.

But it's not just their music that has fans screaming for more. Hanson's trademark shoulder-length blond locks and angelic good looks have girls of all ages (and even grown-up women) swooning all over the globe. Lead singer, Taylor, is the proud owner of a *Smash Hits* award for Most Fanciable Male and all three Hanson brothers are adored by girl fans everywhere. The boys will never know how many millions of kisses they get before they go to bed every night, on posters and magazine cuttings on bedroom walls throughout the world.

But then Hanson are no ordinary band. They are a phenomenon. The three brothers, Isaac (Ike), Taylor (Tay) and Zachary (Zac), were just sixteen, fourteen and eleven respectively when they released their first single. They join an elite club of young brother and sister combos like the Bee Gees and the Jackson 5 (who had their first number one when Michael Jackson was only fourteen, and were the springboard for sister, Janet Jackson) to have conquered the charts. But

Hanson take the biscuit when it comes to age. They are one of the youngest bands ever to top the US chart. In the UK, the last band to boast an eleven-year-old member and reach number one was Musical Youth, fifteen years earlier in 1982.

Whereas many teen sensations are created and controlled by record companies looking for a novelty act, Hanson are totally real. They write and play all the music themselves and were performing as a band years before they even knew what a recording contract was. Compare this with the Spice Girls, who didn't play live until six months after their first album release. Hanson had already chalked up over 300 public performances before most people had even heard of their home town, Tulsa, in Oklahoma. They'll sing live at any opportunity – even in the middle of interviews.

But Hanson don't just write any old songs, they write extremely good ones. Perfectly rounded parcels of pop precision that have earned them respect from all corners of the music industry.

'They have a real flair for writing clever pop and are very knowledgeable about music,' says their manager, Christopher Sabec. 'Sometimes I have to remind myself that they are still kids, because their work and attitude are way beyond their years.'

And London's Capital Radio's David 'Kid' Jensen says, 'They're going to be absolutely massive. They'll be bigger than the Spice Girls. Every now and then an act comes along such as the Jackson Five. Take That didn't come close to the hysteria which surrounded the Jacksons, but Hanson will create that hysteria.'

The Spice Girls and Michael Jackson had better watch out!

Newspapers jumped on the bandwagon straightaway, with *The Times* predicting that Hanson would be superstars for the new millennium and the normally stuck-up *LA Times* declaring that '"MMMBop" is the best single of the year so far.' In Oklahoma, the band even had a special day named after them. To honour 'MMMBop' and *Middle Of Nowhere* reaching number one in America, the governor of the boys' home state pronounced that 6 May would be known as Hanson Day for the rest of history.

But anyone can get lucky with a one-off single if they're in the right place at the right time. The hard part is to follow up a hugely successful debut with more of the same. Hanson did exactly that. These three boys, who still share a bedroom with each other at home (together with their expanding Lego collection), quickly backed up their initial success with the release of their first major album, *Middle Of Nowhere*. A bouncy concoction of jubilant pop, contemporary rock, seventies' soul and tinges of gospel, it too caught the public's imagination at a time when many of the other records in the charts were so depressing.

In the USA, the album sold one million copies in just three weeks to reach the number one spot. In the UK it got to this position in early June 1997, making Hanson the youngest band ever to have a number one album in the UK. That week, Hanson were top of both the singles and albums charts in the UK, USA and Australia – a feat no other band has ever equalled. Current estimates are that over ten million people have bought the album worldwide, making Hanson one of the most successful new artists of all time. Clearly they are no one-hit wonders.

Their record company was so confident in Hanson's ability that they released two videos for the next single 'Where's The Love' (one featuring them playing an acoustic version of the song on MTV). And they were right. It became their second top-ten hit in a row, reaching number four in the UK charts. Hot on its heels, their third single 'I Will Come To You' entered the UK chart at number five and Hanson found themselves on an unstoppable rise to fame that was now out of their control.

Everybody wanted a piece of the action. They appeared on every major American television network (and got asked a few stupid questions, such as, 'How did you meet?') as well as guesting on prestigious US chat shows (often screened after their bedtime!). One of the most famous chat show hosts in the USA, David Letterman, was so blown away by them he said, 'Someone should give these kids their own show.'

Like Letterman, everyone who came into contact with the young boys or saw them on TV was overwhelmed by their sense of fun and down-to-earth honesty. These were three polite, charming boys who had not let their position at the top of the charts go to their heads – and who looked like they were having the time of their lives.

Which, of course, they were. In November 1997, Hanson strengthened their reputation by winning a string of industry prizes. At the MTV Europe awards, they won Best Breakthrough Act and Best Song ('MMMBop') and three weeks later walked off with gongs for Best New Act and Best Single ('MMMBop') at the *Smash Hits* Awards (not forgetting Tay's blush-making Most

Fanciable Male award). This was followed by another MTV award for the most requested video on the channel. Meanwhile, the boys released an hour-long video of their own called *Tulsa, Tokyo And The Middle Of Nowhere*, which charted their phenomenal story, backed up with footage from their sell-out concerts and a home movie that the boys had made themselves.

The month before, the National Milk Promotion Board had been so impressed by their wholesome image and immense appeal that they cast Hanson as the latest in a long line of celebrities advertising milk in a national campaign. Their fee? A cool one million pounds. The boys' pocket money prospects were ertainly looking up.

Hanson's lives became increasingly hectic as they travelled all over the world promoting their album and making guest appearances. In one week in November they flew from Paris to Amsterdam to LA to Miami, presented the MTV awards – and managed to film a half-hour TV show called *Meet Hanson!* But somehow they still found time to release a special album in time for Christmas, *Snowed In*, a series of classic festive songs given that special Hanson twist.

The icing on 1997's cake, though, was meeting American president Bill Clinton and his family when Hanson sang 'Merry Christmas, Baby' as part of a star-studded musical line-up for American TV called *Christmas In Washington*. The excitement over, they finally went home for a well-deserved break before renewing their assault on the world in 1998.

On 25 February, Hanson were nominated for three more awards at America's most prestigious music ceremony, the Grammys – the music world's equivalent of the Oscars. Here they performed live in front of a massive global TV audience of 1.5 billion in over 190 countries. A month later they released 'Weird', the fourth song from *Middle Of Nowhere*, a haunting ballad used in the hit film *The Borrowers*. It had been a whirlwind twelve months and the boys must have looked back and wondered how it all happened. This is what you're about to find out.

CHAPTER TWO

Family Matters

The inseparable Hanson clan are a model family (and not just because of their looks), a shining example of domestic perfection that should be shown around at school – though you certainly wouldn't see them on *EastEnders* or *Grange Hill*. They have been described as the anti-Simpsons – they hardly ever argue, they look out for each other, and despite spending every minute of every day together, they don't seem to get irritable or bored.

Maybe this is due to their Christian upbringing. *Middle Of Nowhere* is dedicated to God (you'll see 'To Him in whom all things find their purpose' written inside the album cover) and the phrase 'God's will' is inscribed on their daily list of chores. The boys are reluctant to talk about their religion, but Ike does say, 'Our faith is important to us. It's something that keeps your head screwed on straight, just like having a good relationship with each other and our family.'

Indeed, their father, Walker Hanson, says that he encouraged his sons to start playing together after he had a message from God. Their mother, Diana, explains, 'The idea for the band came to my husband in a vision during dinner prayer.' Walker saw his sons performing in a concert hall in front of thousands of fans. Now the vision has become reality, although even Walker has been shocked by the speed and scale of his sons' rise to fame. 'We never dreamed it would lead to this,' he says.

While divine intervention is always handy, the role Hanson's parents have played has been just as important as any miracle from above. Walker quit his highly paid job last year to oversee his sons' career ('Nothing is more important than the time you spend with your kids,' he has said) and both parents have been behind their three eldest sons' efforts one hundred per cent.

Their attitude has never been to force the boys into the spotlight or try to live the pop-star lifestyle for themselves through their children, but purely to help them wherever they could.

'There'll be rumours that our mum and dad whip us and make us do this,' says Zac. 'But I've been doing this since I was six. This is what we wanna do.'

'Our parents say we can stop whenever we want,' adds Tay. 'They're on our team. They're not like some record company person who likes you because you're making money for them.'

Parental support goes much further than with other bands. From checking contracts to putting the boys' health and welfare before their career, Walker and Diana are there, making sure they're not out in the cold too long at photoshoots or giving them a lift because they're too young to drive (although Ike has just passed his test).

One crucial reason why Hanson are so close and have been able to dedicate so much time to music is that they have never been to school, and are taught at home by their parents. Walker explains simply, 'We just felt it was better for the kids.'

Exams are taken around the dinner table and then sent off to the local education authority to be marked.

'I don't think we could be the band without home school,' says Zac.

But this system doesn't mean that their studies suffer – far from it. As Tay says, 'Our grades are always good, they average a B – and by working all over the world we are learning more than we ever could by having our heads stuck in a book. We'll read about Notre-Dame and then go to Paris to see it.'

As part of this learning experience, Walker encourages his sons to keep diaries so they'll remember their travels. 'We bring a journal with us all the time,' says Ike. 'We write down everything.'

Home study has also allowed them to go on tour. If they were at school, jokes Tay, 'We'd have to send a lot of notes to our teachers about having to go places.'

Because the brothers spend most of their time with people older than them, they have become more mature than kids their own age. 'Home school means we don't treat each other any differently or see our ages as an issue,' says Zac. 'Our parents treat us like adults and speak to us like adults.' This allows them to cope with the bizarre grown-up world into which they've been thrown.

Even though they are now fully fledged pop stars, there are still no excuses when it comes to school work (they had to study in their dressing room between takes for *TOTP* last year). An average day will see them rehearsing up to four hours, recording TV appearances, giving radio and magazine interviews (they once did twenty-one in one day!), meeting fans and travelling – but their parents still make sure they don't play truant. And that can make life pretty uncomfortable. They get up at six every morning for lessons (they have a maths tutor too) and it's lights out at 10 p.m. Rock 'n' roll!

In between, they still find time for songwriting, checking out their Internet sites to read messages from fans and, says Zac, they like to stop in Segaworld whenever they can. No wonder Ike says that when they get home to Tulsa, all they want to do is 'sleep as much as possible.'

For many older teenage boys, Ike's relationship with his family will appear especially unusual. Many seventeen-year-olds are desperate to get away from their parents and younger brothers. 'People ask us if we fight,' says Ike, 'but really we get along very, very well.' They may playfight and practise karate on each other, but that's as far as it goes.

'We have arguments sometimes – that's just life,' continues Tay, 'but we're basically best friends. We're not like Oasis.' That's for sure – if there was a swear box in the Hanson household it would be empty. 'It's great to be best friends with your brothers,' adds Tay. 'Then you've got friends for life.'

The boys have just got a new friend, in the

tiny shape of Zoe Genevieve Hanson, born on 14 January this year. She joins brother Mackenzie (four) and sisters Avery (seven) and Jessica (nine) as the seventh in the Hanson fold. Every single one of them is blond.

'They're all outgoing in their own way,' says Tay of his fellow siblings, 'and have music in them.'

So could the Hanson trio eventually become the Hanson Seven?

'We're willing to let them in the band,' concedes Zac. 'We've asked them before. But I think they want to do their own thing.'

They asked Jessica if she wanted to play bass – about the only instrument the boys don't play themselves – but she turned them down. 'She's into dancing,' explains Ike.

In fact, the boys are more worried about the younger ones. 'If Avery was in the band, she'd completely take over,' says Tay.

And Zac is keeping an eye on Mac. 'He's got the rhythm. I've got to watch out – he'll steal my place.'

Wherever the boys go in the world, they carry a snowglobe of Tulsa (a present from friends) to remind them of home. 'It's always nice to be able to come back to Tulsa,' says Tay. 'Even though New York and LA and all those different places are cool, Oklahoma is family.'

Home is extremely important for Hanson – not just as a place to sleep, but somewhere to work and play too. Apart from anything, it's their studio. Everywhere you look there are instruments and sheet music lying around and lyrics scribbled on pieces of paper and magazines. This is where most of the Hanson songs have been born, a music factory churning out a never-ending series of chart-busting hits.

But the boys also need time to relax and like nothing better than to hang out in their garage, which has been turned into an art gallery that has murals with storylines drawn all over the walls. They call it the 'den of robbers' because the coloured walls and lights make it look like a gangster's HQ. Tay and Zac are keen cartoon-ists and have left barely an inch uncovered with their doodling.

They have also come up with some pretty bizarre stories, using their much-prized Lego collection to make animations, which they then film. Ike says, 'We did a Batman one which was kind of gruesome. We used a lot of ketchup. It was in an airport and we pushed this guy out of the control tower. And then the Batmobile screeches on to the runway and there's all these henchmen.'

'And they blow away all the passengers in the plane,' continues Tay. Could this be the darker side to Hanson? 'We're just having fun,' replies Tay. So much for being mature.

'Believe me,' says Ike, 'we are not growing up too fast.'

When they're not inside they'll lark around in their garden, where they've set up a football goal and built a treehouse, zoom about on rollerblades (which they take on tour – 'The last time we were in England we got sick because we were rollerblading and it was too cold,' says Ike), or play street hockey or basketball. They've even been waterskiing on a nearby lake. 'We just love sports, period,' says Ike. 'We're never any good,' he adds modestly. Other favourite pastimes include Laserquest, pool, table tennis, dirt bikes, making home movies and the cinema. A bit of a madhouse it would appear. 'Can you imagine what it's like when we're all charging around at home with our brothers, sisters and friends?' asks Ike. 'It's never quiet.'

It's not all play though. Even though they're three of the most famous teenagers in the world and could easily afford to pay someone to do their odd jobs for them, they can't duck out of their chores. 'We don't get special treatment,' confirms Ike.

'We are normal kids,' adds Zac, 'besides the place in the charts.'

Over the next few years, they will encounter all kinds of temptations and lows as well as highs. Thanks to Hanson's stable home life, the future should be equally secure. When Zac was asked how he would cope with fame, he said: 'It all starts out with being sane in the first place.' Ike's main ambition is 'to watch over my younger brothers and carry on enjoying myself.' And, good news for Hanson admirers all over the world, Tay says, 'It's hard to break up, because if we did, we'd see each other every day anyway.'

CHAPTER THREE

The Early Years

How did three teenagers achieve global success and critical acclaim before they were even old enough to shave? Well, practice makes perfect, and Hanson, despite their youth, already had a wealth of experience behind them before they came MMMBopping into our lives. 'It's not like we're these child geniuses, who woke up one morning suddenly able to write great songs,' says Tay. 'We've been snapping our fingers and singing a cappella for as long as we've been able.'

The band first performed live seven years ago (or to put that in perspective, over half of Zac's lifetime) in their hometown. But their story begins even earlier. The boys' parents were both pretty musical themselves. Diana studied music at college and had been a professional singer before becoming a professional mum, and both parents had travelled around America belting out Christian songs with a gospel choir. Walker played guitar and piano for a hobby.

Tay remembers, 'Our mother was always singing around the house. It's in our genes.'

Walker and Diana would lullaby their sons to sleep and soon they were teaching them to sing for themselves, starting with a harmonized amen after grace around the dinner table.

Their parents weren't to know that the boys would take to harmony like most kids take to video games. Before they knew it, the brothers were spending all their time making up their own three-part harmonies and little ditties. Plus they had that special intuitive understanding that can only come when you have the same blood.

'We wouldn't work better with anybody else,' Tay would say later. 'You couldn't do it this young if you weren't brothers.'

Even when they talk, they are on exactly the same wavelength and always finish each other's sentences.

At the time, their father had a highly-paid job in the oil industry, which often took him out of America on business. And as befits such a tight-knit family, he would take the whole Hanson clan with him. Since the boys were taught at home, this didn't affect their schooling. But it was to have a direct impact on Tay, Ike and Zac's continuing musical education.

In 1988, the family left America to spend a year in Venezuela, Trinidad and Ecuador. As the children would not be able to understand the television or radio, Walker invested in a series of yearly music compilations beginning with 1958 and continuing through to 1969. This covered the early years of rock 'n' roll, featuring people such as the Beach Boys, the Jackson Five, the Supremes and, of course, the King himself, Elvis.

Most nights while they were away, their parents would lead the Hanson troupe in sing-songs to those very records, with Walker on guitar. Before long, the eldest Hansons were singing a capella (without any musical accompaniment) versions of these classic hits and these were to form the basics of the music you hear today.

'It was just coincidence that we picked this particular style to take with us,' says Ike. 'But it was very inspirational. It's just great music – all that Chuck Berry, Otis Redding, Aretha Franklin, old Beatles. These people are the origins for what all music is today.'

That year abroad was also important because it brought the family closer together. Without most of the distractions of modern-day living, such as TV and Nintendos, without many friends and unable to communicate with the locals, the Hansons came to rely on each other more, and really bond as a family.

When they returned to America, the brothers soon moved on to writing their own songs. 'It was a natural progression because we were always singing,' says Tay. 'Our parents used to joke that they'd tell us to do the dishes and then they'd come back and we'd have written a song.'

Their folks were pretty tolerant, though – more than just being proud parents, they'd realized that their sons had a real talent. 'They'd tell us, "This better be good",' says Zac, 'and give us a chance to sing it. Then, of course, we'd still have to do the dishes!'

When the boys started, these half-songs and part-melodies were beginning to get that unmistakable Hanson sound, but the subject matter wasn't quite so sophisticated. Naturally, the youngsters were writing about the things that affected them most. 'We wrote a lot of songs about frogs and ants,' laughs Walker.

The funny thing is, if someone in the family had thought to write them down, these early musical efforts might well have become collectors' items. In fact, it was the eldest, Ike, who penned the lyrics to the first Hanson song when he was just eight – calling it 'Rain Falling Down'.

The next piece in the jigsaw fell into place when Ike, and later Tay and Zac, began piano lessons. This wasn't part of any career plan – rather that their mother saw it as an essential part of home schooling. There's no need to tell you who took to the ivories the most naturally – you'll already know from watching Taylor bouncing around behind his keyboard. But learning the piano also gave the brothers another dimension. Now they could write down the music that, until then, had only existed in their overactive imaginations.

Their first public gig came at the end of 1991 at their father's company picnic. The boys were eleven, eight and six. There wasn't quite as much screaming as they are accustomed to now, but the Hanson Brothers, as they were first known, still went down a storm. Before long, their mum was taking bookings for them to sing at private parties and weddings, church events, school assemblies and local restaurants, usually for free. 'We had this thing back in Tulsa where we'd sing in every restaurant we'd go to,' says Tay, 'hoping they'd give us free pizza or something.' Not quite the wild lifestyle we associate with most bands! 'The gigs we played were usually early evening or in the afternoon, so we never had many late nights,' he adds.

In 1992 they begged their parents to let them play in a competition for new acts at the local spring festival, the Mayfest. 'We sang an a capella medley of nineteen-fifties cover versions, wearing leather jackets and sunglasses,' remembers Tay. 'Originally, we would all sort of match – like maybe we'd be colour coordinated. But we said, this is just too corny. We still kind of coordinate the colour, but we really just wear what we want – whatever's comfortable.'

Some say that their present look has helped them appeal to both the teen and the indie market, but the boys have never really thought about it that much. Ike puts it simply, 'What we wear is whatever is clean and in the wardrobe. It's as contrived as that.'

Even at this stage, the boys took their music very seriously, and they practised for four hours a day, five days a week for a month to perfect a thirty-minute unaccompanied set for the contest. The judges were impressed by their musicality, but they didn't win because Hanson were still seen as something of a novelty act – which in many respects they were. Not that Zac minded – he dashed off to play on his skateboard the minute they'd finished. The overwhelming reaction from the public was, 'Aren't they cute?' While they get a similar reaction today, no one can dismiss Hanson quite so easily any more.

But then the boys were in it just to have fun, and over the next few years, that's exactly what they did. As has become patently obvious, they have always loved performing, whether it's on a rickety tumbledown stage in little Tulsa or on the world stage they find themselves on now.

Over the next three years, the boys began to hone their performance skills further, as well as shortening their name from the Hanson Brothers to Hanson. At first, as they didn't play any instruments, they took dance lessons (in the best tradition of boy bands) to liven up their perform-ances. As with everything to do with their sons' music, Walker and Diana took this step very seriously, and converted their front room into a rehearsal space complete with full-length mirrors down one wall.

At these early gigs the boys had their first experience of what has become as much a staple at Hanson concerts as the pop itself – screaming girls. Despite the fact that the boys were sporting short back and sides (the long hair would come later), Hanson-mania was already kicking in. The family were forever picking up the phone to be greeted with 'I love you' screamed down the receiver by gaggles of girl fans. In the end, they had to get an answerphone to screen their calls and install a second ex-directory phone line for friends and family.

Then, in 1994, they had their first big break. The boys were getting increasingly serious about the commercial aspect of their music and pestered their parents to take them to a music convention in Austin, Texas, called South By Southwest, which would be attended by the top dogs in the recording business. This wasn't the first time Hanson had performed outside their own state – they were already getting used to studying in the back of vans and in hotel rooms from New Orleans to LA – but it was the most crucial.

After going up to hundreds of important-looking people (there was no way of knowing who they were – but if someone was wearing a suit it was a start) and asking to sing for them or just hanging around on street corners harmonizing, they began to realize it wasn't going to be easy.

Just as they were giving up hope, they met a young entertainment lawyer and band manager called Christopher Sabec at an outdoor barbecue, who not only took the time to listen, but loved what he heard. 'Where are your parents?' asked Sabec. 'I need to speak to them fast.'

Sabec agreed to do what he could for the band, but he couldn't promise anything. No problem, said the boys, unable to contain their excitement, just do what you can.

Back home, their live shows were pulling in bigger and more fanatical crowds, who would snap up Diana's Hanson T-shirts by the dozen and who began to ask where they could buy a tape of the boys' music. At the time they didn't have one, but the requests were so frequent that in the autumn of 1994, Walker and Diana paid for some backing musicians and studio time and Hanson's debut album *Boomerang* was born. Recorded when the boys were thirteen, ten and eight, it was a classic R & B record. Six of the nine tracks were written by Hanson, the others being covers, notably 'The Love You Save' by the Jackson Five, to whom they've been so often compared.

Almost a year after they had first met him, Sabec happened to be passing through Tulsa and contacted the Hansons to see whether he could pay a quick visit. He caught one of the boys' performances and was blown away by the reaction of the fans. He ended up staying for a fortnight and by the time he left, he was Hanson's manager – official.

But sadly, while *Boomerang* was a big hit with

the fans, it hardly had record company bosses swooning. It behaved rather like a boomerang itself, always winging its way back to them with a rejection slip in tow.

Hanson's musical tastes were changing anyway. The guys were moving away from the clean-cut R & B and swing that was dominating the charts towards more rock-orientated music and they were also getting frustrated at singing along to backing tapes. So Ike got a guitar from a pawn shop, Tay borrowed a keyboard from a friend, and Zac found a drum kit in a friend's attic. They were so desperate to play live that the first gig they did was just one week later. Modest as ever, Tay says, 'That doesn't mean we were good, it just means we got out there and did it.'

Naturally, things didn't always go according to plan – and we're not just talking chords and notes. Tay says, 'When we first started out, Zac had some old Ludwig drums that wouldn't stay still – they would roll across the stage.'

Another time, Zac was sitting on a chest to reach the drums, overbalanced during a solo and fell backwards off the stage to peals of laughter. Ike had his share of problems too – not least when his strap broke and he dropped his guitar mid-song. But that didn't affect their determination.

'Once we got the instruments, we realized this was what we were going to do,' says Ike. 'We wanted to make our music – not just sing it, but play it.'

At first, the dancing was still part of their act. 'We'd switch – we'd play, then dance,' says Tay. But as their instrumental skills progressed, they cut it out altogether and began to concentrate on what they did best.

They performed their first professional gig in the summer of 1995 at the Blue Rose Cafe in Tulsa – a well-respected venue for local talent. The only problem was Hanson couldn't play inside because under American law they were too young to enter somewhere that served alcohol. So a temporary stage was set up in the car park, close to a number of outdoor restaurants. As it turned out, the ban worked in their favour. They were able to attract a much bigger crowd than could have squeezed inside and they were invited back a number of times over the next few months. Cafe owner, Tom Dittus, said, 'We'd feed the kids in the crowd little burgers and soda pop, and they'd sit there mouthing all the words. It was the cutest thing in the world.'

The band were so encouraged, they returned to the studio at the end of 1995 to record their new, more complete sound on a fifteen-song album entitled *MMMBop*. They weren't short of material – they'd already penned over 100 songs. Their biggest problem was forcing Zac to sit still, and they had to take video-game breaks every two hours to keep him happy.

The boys composed all the music themselves and played every instrument except for bass. The album included an early version of 'MMMBop', but the birth of the song had actually come even earlier, while the guys were working on backing vocals for *Boomerang*.

'It was written over a year,' says Ike. 'We would be walking around the house and we would go, "Remember that background part from the album? Let's sing that." Then we would go into it and we'd be, like, "Oh man, that sounds really cool."'

Still, they had to make a decision on how to spell it. But that was easy. 'It wasn't quite MMMMMMMMMBop,' explains Ike, 'and it wasn't quite MBop. It was "MMMBop".'

'MMMBop' isn't just a catchy chorus – like all of Hanson's songs, it's steeped in meaning too. 'It's about friendships,' says Tay. 'The first verse says: "You have so many relationships in this life/Only one or two will last/You're going through all this pain and strife/Then you turn your back and they're gone so fast." It's deeper than it sounds.'

An even older song, which didn't make it to the album, was equally sophisticated, telling the story of two dolls on the mantelpiece above the fire – a one-armed soldier and a one-legged ballerina – that fall into the flames and melt together so they'll never be lonely.

Not only was their songwriting improving, the charts were changing too. It seemed the public had had enough of depressing songs and wanted tunes that they could hum along to, songs that would cheer them up and take them away from the drudgery and boredom of everyday life.

Hanson had already been turned down by an astonishing fourteen major record labels, including their home now, Mercury Records, and as Tay's voice came close to breaking, the band thought they were past it. 'We thought it would happen when we were younger,' says Tay. 'We were saying, "Man, we're too old."'

But as the musical climate changed, so would their luck.

CHAPTER FOUR

Big Deal

MMMBop was to launch Hanson to the top. Not the single that we all know and love, but that second independent album changed the boys' lives irreversibly and turned them into stars. Little did they know it at the time, but in just over a year they wouldn't be able to walk down the street without being mobbed.

Record companies were worried about the decreasing sales of grunge and rap and were looking for a new style. 'For a while, there was that alternative thing, and it was huge,' explains Tay. 'And now it's coming back to music being fun. Not corny, but enjoyable. Not down-and-out "I hate my life."'

In early 1996 their manager, who for so long had been banging his head against a brick wall, suddenly found that his phone wouldn't stop ringing. This was sweet revenge for Sabec. For the past year his friends and colleagues had been telling him he was mad. 'Most record labels advised me to get away from this act as fast as possible,' Sabec admitted after he first took up their case. When those very same people heard 'MMMBop' it was a different story.

Although Hanson were attracting a lot of interest, no one offered them a recording contract until Sabec, almost out of desperation, played the album to his girlfriend. As luck would have it, she happened to be an executive at Mercury, and she passed it on to the label's vice-president in New York, Steve Greenberg, who was so impressed he thought someone was trying to pull the wool over his eyes.

This was the final stumbling block Hanson still had to overcome. The teenagers were so good that people didn't believe it was their own work. The songwriting was so mature and harmonies so professional that record companies who were used to pre-packaged teen groups were convinced that some grown-ups were involved.

'I was convinced it was fake,' admitted Greenberg, when he first heard the tape. 'I was sure there was some adult pulling the strings, or the vocals were manipulated and they weren't really playing their instruments.'

Throughout Hanson's career, such accusations have been constantly thrown at the band. Tay has learnt to live with it. 'People are going to say, "Oh, they're young kids, they don't play, they don't write, they were put together – something's got to be screwy about that",' he says. 'But you just have to listen to the music – it speaks for itself.'

And that's exactly what Greenberg did. He got on a plane and went to see them with his own eyes in Coffeyville, Kansas. Hanson still think they didn't play very well that day.

'The audience didn't get into it,' says Tay. 'It was one of those shows where you go, "Why did he have to come to this?"'

But he needn't have worried – Greenberg was over the moon. 'They played great, they sang great, they completely recreated the music on the tape live,' he says. 'And they did it all themselves, there wasn't an adult in sight.'

Greenberg was more or less convinced that he would sign Hanson, but first he wanted to get to know them better to make sure he wasn't making a mistake. So a few weeks later he flew to Tulsa to visit the family. They took him to a local adventure park, where they went go-karting and got soaked on the bumper boats. 'That was great fun, but it's very different,' admitted Greenberg. 'You probably don't do that when you're signing Pearl Jam.'

When he left, he was convinced the boys not only had real talent, but that they also had the personality to win over army upon army of fans. Hanson were signed for a six-album deal, such was the confidence Mercury had in the boys. This was certainly no one-off gamble.

Greenberg wanted to get them into the studio – and fast. Hanson were suffering from a fate that not many of today's bands will ever have to contend with – Tay's voice was breaking.

'We literally rushed them to LA,' says Greenberg. '"Get in a van! Let's get to LA as soon as possible."'

Thanks to the excellence of the record's producers, it is impossible to tell that Tay's voice got deeper during the five months from July to November 1996 it took them to record the album. 'We had to lower some of the songs, but that's the way life goes,' says Tay matter-of-factly. 'If you listen closely, you'll hear my voice is about four notes lower at the end of the album than it was at the beginning.'

While Greenberg was confident in the boys' ability, he also realized that teen acts aren't always taken seriously by people and he wanted to put that right straight away. 'They needed to be around people who could help them make the right kind of record,' he says. 'Many people who have dealt with kids on records have taken a fairly condescending approach and made very young-sounding records. The music the Hansons had written demanded greater care.'

So he persuaded the mega-hip Dust Brothers (the US equivalent of the Chemical Brothers), who had produced Beck's prize-winning album *Odelay,* and producer and arranger Steve Lironi, who had worked with Black Grape and Space, to work behind the mixing desk. He also drafted in a clutch of expert songwriters (including, bizarrely, Beck's dad, who did the string arrangements) to help perfect it. These people were the best in the business – between them they had worked with the Righteous Brothers, Bon Jovi, Aerosmith, Belinda Carlisle and The Beatles – and their age and experience were the perfect complement to Hanson's youth and exuberance.

For the brothers, this was somewhat unusual. They had spent their entire lives as part of such a close-knit gang and their music had always been pure Hanson – free of outside influences. Suddenly they had to work with people they'd never even met. 'At first it was strange,' says Tay, 'because we didn't know what it was going to be like. But once we got in there, most of the people were very easy to work with.'

Ike adds that Beck's dad 'was a very nice guy, he looks a lot like Beck.'

'He's Beck in twenty-five years,' jokes Zac. 'Beck with wrinkles.'

More than anything, they were flattered that these people wanted to work with them. 'We were amazed that such well-known writers were willing to write with an unknown band on their debut,' says Tay.

The boys were particularly impressed with the Dust Brothers. 'It was cool meeting them,' says Tay. 'We recorded stuff in their house and messed around in their pool.'

'They added some interesting elements that we might not have thought of,' adds Ike. '"MMMBop" is a good example. They added a "ruh-uh-ruh-uh-ruh-uh-ruh" thing.'

The homely atmosphere at the Dust Brothers' studio was almost more important than their musical input. After the initial surprise that they didn't live up to their name ('I was surprised . . . they're not really dusty,' says Tay. 'They have a very clean house,' adds Zac), the laid-back atmosphere provided the perfect working environment for the young boys.

'We did a photo shoot where we jumped into

their swimming pool with all our clothes on,' says Ike. 'Long pants, really baggy. Zac was the first one to jump.'

'The problem is that you start drowning,' adds Zac, obviously yet to take his swimming proficiency test and learn how to tread water wearing pyjamas! Photo shoot or not, it seems that this was a pretty regular occurence. 'Zac played the drums soaking wet on one song,' says Tay.

Another highlight during the recording of the album was chatting on the phone with Steve Tyler from Aerosmith, one of Hanson's favourite bands, after he happened to phone up while they were there. Later, in April 1997, they would actually get to meet their hero, an event that Hanson describe as 'their biggest buzz'. The guys also took advantage of living near the beach and went surfing at every opportunity.

But it wasn't all larking around. The boys had the serious job of putting together a hit record. Zac, who can always be relied on to say something incredibly sensible when you least expect it, says, 'It's a lot of work. Once you get a record deal, it doesn't stop there!'

Mercury wanted to make sure that, in keeping with the Hanson philosophy, *Middle Of Nowhere* was a real family effort. So although Tay has the most rounded and expressive voice, both Ike and Zac were given some songs too. Consequently, Ike fronts the ever-so-romantic 'A Minute Without You' and Zac takes the lead on 'Man From Milwaukee' and 'Lucy' – inspired by the girl in the *Snoopy* cartoon.

The end result is a perfect piece of feel-good pop that appeals to all ages. Four songs were written solely by Hanson. Three of these were taken from their second independent album *MMMBop* – 'Thinking Of You', 'With You In Your Dreams' and, surprise surprise, 'MMMBop' – and the other was the CD bonus track, 'Man From Milwaukee'. Even though the album had some input from outside sources, its best selling point is that it's more or less all Hanson's work. The harmonies they learnt from all those sixties' records remain as the centrepiece.

'Harmony is a very, very large part of Hanson,' says Ike. 'It's the base of our music style.'

'We're perceived as cool because we are real,' adds Tay. 'It's not like some manager came along and put us together. We love doing this so there is no effort involved in the way we look or sound, and I think people can tell we're not phoney.'

The millions of people who bought their single certainly didn't think they were phoney.

As soon as 'MMMBop' was released, it was clear it was heading straight for the top of the charts. The boys had been asked many times how they would celebrate if they got to number one and they came out with a variety of crazy answers. Ike joked he'd 'Go on some hot date,' or 'Have a party with all my friends from home.' Tay said he'd 'Jump up and down' and Zac said, 'Get a girlfriend' before changing his mind to 'Go to Laserquest and play, like, fifty times.' In the end, Zac was more or less right – they went to a games arcade, although Zac didn't get to stay as long as he wanted. 'We played a few games and then they kicked us out,' says Tay.

The video for 'MMMBop' wasn't filmed until February 1997, and nowhere near as much work went into it as the album, but then that provided a great deal of the appeal. Much like their music, it was completely natural. Just three boys doing what they like best – rollerblading, mucking around on the beach, and generally fooling around.

After discussions with video director Tamra Davis, who had previously worked with Sonic Youth and Luscious Jackson, Hanson decided to go for a home movie feel, even though the video was actually shot in LA. Almost all the ideas for the shoot came from Hanson. Davis had originally suggested that they ride bikes at the start, but the teenagers thought that would be too childish and they ended up catching a taxi instead. The part that Hanson enjoyed the most – rollerblading – nearly didn't happen at all.

'We had twenty minutes of daylight left,' says Ike.

'It just happened that the cameraman knew how to skateboard,' continues Zac.

So he just followed them around, filming on a skateboard. And the bit where Zac and Tay bash into each other was a real accident too. Tay says, 'We both looked back to see the camera. Right before we looked forward again, we suddenly collided. It was a weird coincidence that happened to really work.'

Other video facts: it was freezing on the beach but the boys had to pretend it was summer; the flower that forms the backdrop in certain scenes is now displayed in their garage; and the car that Hanson pretend to drive had been used by Sandra Bullock in the film *Speed 2*: Cruise Control.

The video was to prove just as important to 'MMMBop' hitting number one as the song itself. MTV began airing it straight away in March, a month before the single was released. Ike says that they were surprised they even got on MTV. 'We didn't think people would think we were cool enough,' he says modestly. But the public loved the video and rang up in their droves to request it. Before long, it was number one on MTV and a whole host of other video channels in America and Canada.

'We're all totally blown away by the way people have responded,' says Ike. 'The scary thing was how fast it happened. It's incredible to think your song could be in the top forty, much less number one. We were totally like, "Wow, how did that happen?"'

'How do you describe seeing something that you just wrote sitting at home, in the charts,' continues Tay.

'Michael Jackson is like two notches below you,' adds Ike, 'and that's when you go, "That's weird."'

'Pinch me,' says Zac.

'Yeah, somebody smack me really hard,' says Ike.

The chances of someone doing that to any member of the cutest pop group in the world are nil. Kisses, yes. Marriage proposals, yes. But punches? You'd have a better bet on Peter Andre keeping his shirt on.

CHAPTER FIVE

Cool as Ike

FACT FILE

Date of Birth   17 November 1980
Star sign   Scorpio
Nicknames   Ike, Leader, Chewbacca (from *Star Wars*)
Fave colour   Green
Fave ice cream Vanilla

INTERNET RUMOURS
Here's what the latest stories on the Internet claim – could they be true?

Ike says that Pamela Anderson is cute but he prefers Jennifer Aniston; he almost drowned once when a wave knocked him off his surfboard; he names his guitars after girls he has crushes on; he hates getting up before 11 a.m.; and his favourite TV shows are *Seinfeld* and *Beavis and Butthead*.

★

The boys are over the moon when they scoop Best Breakthrough Act and Best Song at the MTV Europe Awards.

There's nothing Hanson like better than playing live (National Tennis Center, New York).

Guesting on the famous *Today* show in the USA doesn't faze our Tay one bit.

Aaah . . . Zac takes time out for a spot of (very cute) daydreaming.

Mixing with the stars: the boys get to meet Lisa-Marie, daughter of the King of Rock 'n' roll, Elvis Presley.

Don't mention girlfriends when Zac's around – though Ike and Tay take the subject a bit more seriously.

The boys take
a welcome
break during
yet another TV
appearance.

Looking slightly lost without their instruments, Hanson put a brave face on . . .

As the eldest, Clarke Isaac Hanson is the most sensible brother and the born leader. But while he is ever protective of the other two, he is never dominating and is perfectly content to let them have their say – although often he doesn't have much choice – and all decisions about the band are taken entirely democratically.

He is the most self-confident and assured Hanson, completely positive about what they are doing, often in the face of fierce criticism. 'We don't worry about what other bands are doing,' he says. 'We do what we do. And they do what they do. Some people make fun of Hanson,' he adds. 'But you know what? I don't give a rip.'

He rarely gets ruffled and always has the energy to cheer up his less-patient younger brothers when they're bored or depressed. He can reel off a whole host of comedy voices and impressions, favourites being Kermit the Frog, Butthead and Louis Armstrong.

'He's cool because he's the older brother he's always been,' says Tay.

Zac even describes him as the 'goofiest member', but Ike thinks that times have changed.

'I used to be the crazy one,' he says, 'but then Zac took over.'

And here is the paradox about Ike – he may

43

be the most grown up, but he can also be just as crazy as his brothers. He'll lark around in interviews with the other two and show off in front of girls, but as the most business-minded of the group, he'll always bring conversations back to the point and the younger brothers will follow his lead.

Ike is also the most sensitive Hanson, a side that first became obvious when the family moved to South America. Ike developed a mystery rash because he missed his best friend so much.

He's earnest and good-natured and lists intelligent conversation and candlelit dinners as some of his favourite ways to spend time. 'I'm a bit of an arty type and very romantic,' he says. And, because he's the oldest, Ike is the one most interested in girls.

'Ike's a girl charmer,' says Zac. 'He's the one who would, like, dedicate songs to people. He's always wanting to be loved by a girl.'

Ike agrees. 'I can't wait for it to happen,' he says. 'It must be an incredible feeling. I've thought about dating a few girls, but being on the road means we would never see them,' he says. 'A girl would probably not want to deal with me.'

There's probably thousands of girls out there who would faithfully wait for years to gaze into Ike's sweet brown eyes.

But there's another condition for any potential girlfriend. 'It would be important for someone to understand how much our music means to us,' says Ike. 'Our music comes first now and hopefully forever.'

Ike is looking for understanding and companionship – not just a short fling, but a long-term relationship. 'It's not just what they look like,' he says, 'it's whether we like them or not. But if they're hot it's always a benefit.'

A major benefit of Hanson's fame for Ike was meeting the hottest girl of them all, Cindy Crawford. 'She's absolutely awesome,' he gushes. 'She's really, really pretty. All three of us met her at a party and she's stayed in our minds ever since.'

Ike's past relationships are a bit of a mystery. 'I've been close a couple of times,' he admits. 'My lifestyle is kinda crazy and often girls just end up being friends instead of girlfriends.'

But Tay has a few secrets up his sleeve after sneakily reading Ike's diary. Apparently, Ike had written that he kissed a girl while they were watching *The 101 Dalmatians* – and she ran home crying to her mum!

There's also a story on the Internet that Ike fancied a girl he met at a Hanson concert, but his parents didn't want him to get involved because he was too young. Ike ignored them and got into trouble when he and the girl were caught holding hands.

One thing is certain about Ike's affections – he's in love with his camcorder. 'It looks cool and I love technical things with a lot of buttons,' he says. 'I'd be really upset if we lost any of the film because it's full of fond memories. Like the time we caught Tay snoozing at the studio.'

Ike's compassionate side comes through in his songwriting too and he writes most of the ballads. 'Just because we're young doesn't mean we don't have emotions,' he says.

He is extremely gifted musically, with a high, soulful voice. He hardly ever lets his guitar leave his side, to the annoyance of Tay, who moans that he's always fiddling around on it. But then Ike's not going to take any notice of Tay, just as he doesn't take any notice of the band's critics.

That same attitude comes through in his mature acceptance of having to wear braces (the only other person ever to wear them while being at number one is Shaznay from All Saints). They were fitted in 1995 and although they're clear and unobtrusive, it still must be embarrassing to wear them in front of millions of people. So far, his younger brothers have escaped. 'Oh, how lucky I am . . . not,' jokes Ike.

Strangely, Ike is much more vain about his hair and Tay once got so annoyed with him describing a past hairstyle during a live-TV interview that he shouted, 'Ike, who *cares* about your hair?'

Hair, music and girls are far from the only focus in Ike's life. Like his brothers, he's a keen sportsman, but he is also a talented writer and has been working on a science-fiction novel for the last three years (not surprisingly, his two favourite school subjects are English and Science). He also likes to write letters, and wasn't very pleased when Tay ruined one he was writing to a female friend by adding, 'I want you desperately' at the bottom.

Tay and Ike are always playing tricks on each other. Once, when they were younger, Tay poured a bottle of glue over Ike's head – he had to shave all his hair off to get rid of it! Luckily Ike's dark-blond curly locks grew back no problem.

Despite these episodes the two remain best friends. However, they don't share the same taste in food, Ike tending to be more refined. He'll look forward to a good steak and loves Italian food such as spaghetti and lasagne as well as Tex-Mex stuff, although he does have a strange habit of eating salt as an appetizer while waiting for his meal to arrive. That's when he's not biting his fingernails.

Despite his other interests, Ike is totally dedicated to Hanson's cause. When asked what he would do with all his money, he replied, 'I'd get a couple more guitars.' And it's only when pushed that he'll let himself go a little. 'I've always wanted a trampoline – a big trampoline,' he says.

Now that he's passed his driving test, he'd like to buy a Corvette or a Jeep Cherokee. But all these distractions come second to the music. When he was asked what he wanted for his seventeenth birthday, he said, 'Our own tour. A full, ninety-minute set of our own songs. Because that's what it's all about, really, playing our music.'

STAR QUALITIES

As a Scorpio, Ike has the most forceful personality of the three brothers and usually likes to take charge. He is a careful and enthusiastic worker whose curiosity and creativity could lead to big success and innovation either in the field of music, or in any other path he may follow. He loves a challenge, especially a physical one, and he has the potential to become an excellent sportsman. Ike also likes to challenge his brain and enjoys activities that really make him think. However, he must be careful not to spread his talents too thinly or he might miss out on excellence in one specific area. He will only make friends with people he thinks he can trust, but those people will remain friends for life. Scorpios are naturally attractive to the opposite sex, but it is important for Ike to channel his high emotional energy in positive directions. His perfect partners are Cancer, Pisces or Aries girls.

CHAPTER SIX

Taylor Made

FACT FILE

Date of Birth	14 March 1983
Star sign	Pisces
Nicknames	Tay, Tayles (because of the braid in his hair), Blondie
Fave colour	Red
Fave ice cream	Strawberry

INTERNET RUMOURS

Here's what the latest stories on the Internet claim — could they be true?

Tay is supposed to have stolen a Transformer from a friend when he was younger and Ike told their parents, saying that Tay got a new toy from nowhere; he wears CKBe aftershave; Tay and Zac have weekly arm-wrestling competitions and Tay always wins; he says that Pamela Anderson is fit, Baby Spice is pretty cute and he likes

Jennifer Aniston; he loves mashed potatoes; and his favourite films are *Star Wars* and *The Hunchback Of Notre Dame*.

Jordan Taylor Hanson is the most popular member of the band with the female fans and it's not difficult to see why. Lead singers are often the main target of girls' affections, no matter what they look like. But with Tay they have got good reason. His deep-blue eyes, sandy-blond hair, warm smile and sexy lip curl are made all the more attractive by a highly charged, plaintive singing voice that can reduce even the most cold-hearted listener to tears.

He has often been compared to a young Michael Jackson (presumably for his musical ability rather than his looks), and was once even likened to Uma Thurman, thanks to his almost-feminine features! He is regularly mistaken for a girl, something that used to rile him, but now he sees the funny side. 'If I was a girl, I'd feel really sorry for myself because I am ugly,' he jokes, although most of his fans wouldn't agree.

Fame has had little effect on him either, perhaps because he spends so much time in his own little world. 'Tay's a real daydreamer,' says Ike. 'He often just drifts off.'

Maybe this habit has contributed to his appeal

– he has an air of mystery, partly enhanced by his shyness, which makes him all the more alluring. Girls are also attracted to his modesty, which remains despite the fact that he has achieved so much so young.

When embarrassed, Tay can't help himself from going bright red. Mischievous little Zac has picked up on this and annoys Tay by trying to make him blush as much as possible! But Tay will try his hardest not to be singled out (he has often declared: 'The thing that makes us Hanson is there are three guys who sing') and is keen to play himself down. He'd much rather perform than sit around talking about himself.

But while Tay may be shy and distant at first ('I am the quietest one,' he admits), once you get to know him, he is chatty and amusing and will often give the most considered and well-thought-out answers to questions put to the band, especially about his beloved music.

'Tay's the perfectionist of the group,' announces Zac, and even Tay admits he's 'a bit of an intense guy' (a favourite quote is the very deep, 'You have to like yourself before you can do anything.').

His ability to keep things in perspective and his willingness to listen have turned Tay into the peacemaker of the band, even of the family. When anyone has a problem they will come to him for advice. In age, as well as problem-solving, he really finds himself stuck in the middle.

But Tay is not all serious – far from it – and he can and often does 'out-Zac' Zac himself! Tay really is a cross between the other two brothers, a perfect mix of Zac's craziness and Ike's sensitivity.

Tay's charisma and effortless ability to win over countless female fans have inevitably led to talk of him going solo in the future. But he's totally devoted to his brothers and won't even consider that prospect. For Tay, the only thing in his mind that deserves more attention than his brothers is, of course, his music. He's highly creative and totally driven – that you can tell at a glance from his performances. He'll lose himself on stage and bounce around to the music so much that you fear he might do himself an injury (in fact, during a concert in Germany, Tay got so carried away that he chipped a tooth on his microphone and had to be whisked off to the dentist).

Tay and his keyboard have been inseparable ever since he first got his talented hands on it and, more recently, he has also been keen to develop other aspects of his musical repertoire. He already plays the bongos on stage, and off stage he is a keen percussionist. 'I tap on every-thing all the time,' says Tay. 'I like to imagine

I'm playing the drums but it annoys everyone.' He is also having singing lessons to cope with the fact that his voice is breaking.

Wherever he goes he'll carry a dictaphone with him so as not to miss a moment of inspiration and he'll listen to all kinds of music, always leaving himself open to new ideas. His favourite recent single was actually Chumbawamba's 'Tubthumping' ('It's a really cool song,' he says), which is about as far removed from Hanson's melodious sound as it is possible to get.

When Tay does allow himself some time away from his music, you're just as likely to find him reading. His favourite school subject is English Literature and he is very cultured for his age, already having developed a love of Shakespeare and poetry. He's also a big fan of the theatre, especially plays involving ghosts or fantasy characters. He excels at art and while he has as much enthusiasm as Zac for cartoons, his real talent is drawing portraits. His impressions are spot on, and it is seen as a real honour if Tay asks to do your portrait – he only draws people he likes. If he wasn't one of the most lusted-after singers in the world, he would probably have made a living using his artistic talents as either an architect or an interior designer.

When not being so cultured, Tay will watch

one of his favourite TV programmes, *Friends* ('one of the funniest shows ever'), *Frasier* or *Seinfeld,* and pig out on junk food. They say the way to a man's heart is through his stomach and if you are interested in Tay, maybe you could lure him with a 'gigantic quadruple burger with tons of cheese, loads of gunk and huge heaps of fries.'

Tay's a pizza freak too and had a great time in Italy last year. 'For the food and for the girls,' he adds! Hanson's busy schedule takes its toll on the boys and they often need something to keep them going, to keep them awake even. So to wash down his food, Tay will drink coffee. 'We have more caffeine than most adults,' he admits.

The sexiest Hanson's wardrobe is packed full of V-necks and big clumpy boots, and you'll always find four or five necklaces (which he collects) dangling around his chest. Something Tay tries to conceal though is his bleeper. He needs it now he's so in demand, but he's not one to show off about it, and tries to hide it on his waist.

Like younger brother Zac, Tay's been in the wars a bit – thanks to his manically sporty lifestyle. The worst injury he ever had was a broken arm when he was twelve. He was riding his bike down a huge hill and saw his parents coming towards him in their car. He tried to stop but flipped over the handlebars right in front of his mum and dad. He's also got a scar on the back of his leg from playing football, another on his back from rollerblading, and a third just below his left eye from when Ike accidentally pushed him through a glass door when he was little. He has a bad habit of biting his lip too, but fortunately he hasn't done himself any damage yet.

If he did, there'd be a never-ending line of girls queuing up to kiss it better. But Tay doesn't have a girlfriend yet. Times have changed since he used to throw tomatoes at girls when he was a kid, but still he's happy enough as he is at the moment.

'Girls are great, but then so is hanging out with your brothers,' says Tay. 'One day we'll all feel different, but right now girls and kissing aren't high on my list.'

If they were, his dream date would be with Cameron Diaz. He also admits, 'My girlfriend would have to be tender, romantic and faithful, like me.' Tay finds it difficult to meet sincere girls because a lot of the time they're only after him because he's famous. Plus, there's little chance of a decent conversation. 'Some of them are too fanatical, and they scream so much you just can't talk to them,' he says. So if you ever get the chance to meet Tay, try not to get too carried away . . .

He has yet to kiss anyone, but then he's too dedicated to all his fans to concentrate his affections on just one. 'We meet fans and sign auto-graphs,' says Tay, who loves to ask them which songs they like best, 'but if you tell them you have a girlfriend, it's like, "Oh bummer". It's better for us to be single.'

STAR QUALITIES

Pisceans tend to underestimate themselves, although Tay is encouraged by his supportive family. He is very giving, always willing to make sacrifices for others and would be ideally suited to a career in which he could help other people – which could, of course, be music. He is thoughtful, fascinated by the unknown and extremely creative, but he can be easily dis-tracted. He can also be a bit careless with money. Tay will fall in love very easily and could come across as selfish for trying to hurry relationships, but he is sensitive enough to realize this before it is too late. He will be a thoughtful, spon-taneous and caring boyfriend who will expect the same in return and consequently could often be disappointed. He will shower his partner with gifts, but does not like to be taken for granted. His ideal partner would be a Scorpio, who would respond to such flattery, or a Virgo, as she would have the patience to allow him to grow intellec-tually and emotionally, which will take time.

CHAPTER SEVEN

Zany Zac

FACT FILE

Date of birth	22 October 1985
Star sign	Libra
Nicknames	Zac, Prozac, Psycho Boy and Animal (after the drummer in *The Muppets*)
Fave colour	Blue
Fave ice cream	Chocolate

INTERNET RUMOURS

Here's what the latest stories on the Internet claim – could they be true?

He always carries a pack of chewing gum with him; his favourite drink is Dr Pepper; he calls Ike Ikeypoos; and he'd like to have a reptile as a pet. Zac has also been compared to Bart Simpson, and a young Jim Carrey.

★

Like the characters he loves to draw, Zachary Walker Hanson is almost a cartoon himself. He dashes about like someone has put a stick of dynamite in his trousers, bouncing off walls and shouting gibberish. But despite his apparent lack of concentration, he can also be shockingly profound with his own brand of off-the-wall humour and sense of logic.

When he was asked whether he thought Hanson's music might not be taken seriously because they were so young, he replied, 'Think of us as old people with high voices.' And when asked on *The O-Zone*, 'Do you want to be like Michael Jackson?' he came back with the lightning-quick response, 'I like my face the way it is!'

He is also, like all the brothers, surprisingly modest. 'I'm not a great drummer,' says Zac, 'but everybody says I can play, so I'll take their word for it. The secret is, nobody else's arms are as long. I couldn't play guitar or piano, so I went straight to the drums because I have long arms.' He started drumming on pots and pans when he was only four and got his first drum kit when he was nine.

Despite this reluctance to sing his own praises, critics claim that Zac is the most musically gifted of the three. He certainly doesn't miss any opportunity to practise – he will grab anything in sight and start bashing out a rhythm or rehearsing drum rolls. 'I bang on things,' he says simply.

But Zac is not just a little drummer boy who takes his Power Rangers with him everywhere he goes – even the recording studio. He is also an extremely talented songwriter and singer and, after years of classical piano lessons, is now learning to play the bass.

The youngest Hanson insists he only joined the band because his brothers didn't sound any good without him. 'Two-part harmony didn't sound right, so they needed a third person,' he jokes.

Ike, however, implies that they didn't give Zac a choice. 'Zac kind of got stuck.'

He certainly makes the most of his position as the timekeeper though, and likes to stamp his authority on the band.

'Zac is very stubborn,' says Tay. 'He'll go, "I'm the drummer, I'll do whatever I want." He'll speed us up, slow us down, whatever.'

The popular image of Zac is as an irrepressible bundle of energy, the most outgoing of the bunch. He'll wear the most outrageous clothes – one outfit included yellow satin parachute pants and matching yellow platform trainers – and sometimes he puts his hair in dreads. He'll get carried away in interviews and be told off by his brothers. And on the rare occasions that no one's asking him questions, he'll become impatient and start acting up. During a Hanson interview on MTV, after being silent for a couple of minutes, he suddenly shouted, 'You know, *I'm* not talking here.' Later on, when the situation didn't improve, he pretended to fall asleep!

He's also the most hyper on stage, always bantering with the audience and geeing them up – as if that was really necessary. Tay says, 'Zac's wild and he keeps the fans on their toes. He loves to drive 'em crazy.'

During one concert, when Hanson were handing out T-shirts, one little girl was too shy to come up, so Zac went down into the audience and brought her up to the stage himself.

Drummers are typically the most outrageous members of any band, and Zac is no exception, but he's still not old enough to get up to any of the crazy antics that drummers are renowned for. He can't understand why anyone would want to drink beer for a start. But he has been known to 'gently trash' his hotel room with a feather-filled pillow, so maybe that's the first step along the road to rock legend.

But there's another less well-known side to the twelve-year-old tearaway. Tay says, 'You'll kind of know when he's in the room. But sometimes he'll just disappear and you'll find him on his own, drawing.'

Zac agrees, although you never quite know whether he's joking: 'I'm the only one who really knows what I am. I'm quiet,' he says.

'It's kind of funny,' says Tay, 'because Zac's kinda like in control of what he's saying.'

'He'll string people along,' continues Ike. 'He's quite quiet at home but then when he's on stage or he's performing for people he's definitely very hyper. It's just his personality.'

Being so hyper can be a bit of a liability and Zac's had his fair share of injuries. He once broke his nose twice in one year. 'We were wrestling on the floor and Zac banged his nose on a chair,' says Ike, 'and then the second time we were playing on a seesaw –'

'And you stick a rock on one end and you go, "Boom!"' interrupts Zac, pretending to jump down on a seesaw, still bizarrely enthusiastic about the whole episode despite the fact that when Tay hit the other end, the rock went straight into his face. 'There was blood everywhere,' says Zac.

You'd never tell from looking at him now. He has perfect features. His piercing hazel eyes and rounded lips stand out from an impossibly cute face framed by a shock of sandy-blond hair.

The first time Zac saw his face on TV, he said, 'Look at the cute girl – no wait, it's me.'

But while he may get confused by his appearance, his opinions are anything but confused. Despite being so young, he is very sure of himself. When asked 'Which Spice Girl would you be?', he replied, 'I'd rather be . . . Zac. I'm going to be . . . Zac.'

Even though he is so self-assured, he can also get scared, especially in front of the massive crowds that Hanson attract, and he'll look to his older brothers for protection. When he was younger he once ran off stage crying, and another time before a gig, he got so nervous that he threw up.

When he's not performing or being sick, he'll spend most of his time drawing – if he forgets his sketchpad he'll use whatever is at hand, from ketchup and paper plates to his arms – or playing video games.

'Sometimes I plug my Nintendo into the hotel room before I've unpacked anything else,' says Zac. 'It's like I can't live without beating Taylor at NBA Jams.'

'Zac's the best at video games,' admits Tay.

'He kills us,' adds Ike.

'That's because I've been playing since I was three,' says Zac, a computer and technology freak. This is borne out in lessons, where his best subject is maths (apart from creative spelling, he jokes) and his taste in films, two of his favourites being *Men In Black* and *Star Wars*.

Other top pastimes include dropping water bombs on people and collecting miniature shampoo bottles from hotels around the world. Judging from all the travelling the boys have been doing, he must have quite an extensive collection.

Zac's party piece of talking while burping probably wouldn't endear him to the opposite sex, but he still attracts thousands of admirers. At the moment, though, he's not remotely interested. 'What's the point of getting a girlfriend when you're only twelve?' he once said.

Zac's still too young to understand the hysteria that Hanson have created ('Why do girls scream? We need to know,' he asks), but he does realize that their manic lifestyle would make having a girlfriend difficult – 'You'd only see her for a couple of minutes every two years. "Hi! OK, Bye!"'' he says. But there is hope. Zac once cracked in yet another round of questions about girlfriends and said: 'Maybe someday.'

A hot tip for anyone prepared to wait, he 'prefers girls to look natural'. So ditch the make-up when Zac's around.

Apart from flying to the moon or Mars, Zac's only ambition at the moment is to keep on making music. 'I've had this job since I was six so I think I'll carry on for quite a while yet,' he reasons.

Whatever he does, it's certain to make him a rich man. So what would he most like to buy in the whole world? 'A drum store,' he says. But he wouldn't be able to bear actually selling any of them. 'That would be the hard part because I wanna be able to use all of them,' he explains. 'Then again if I got ten million arms I could. Maybe just a huge drum set, like twenty billion-feet high. I don't know.' Either that, or he'd 'give everyone in the world a puppy. Because puppies make you feel good.'

The most important thing in Zac's life though, undoubtedly, is his brothers. 'We're always around each other, even when we don't have to be,' he says. And in irresistibly charming Zac-speak: 'They're like my best friends, only bester.'

STAR QUALITIES

While Librans come across as very level-headed, in reality Zac has to work hard to achieve this. His natural charm and his ability to make decisions quickly and accurately will guarantee him success in his chosen profession and his chart indicates a long and successful career in music. He is capable of working hard for months on end with great attention to detail, so long as he has a good break afterwards. He is immensely moved by human suffering and, like Tay, may dedicate part of his life to helping others. He will have many friends, who will know always to expect the unexpected when he's around. He will be drawn towards long-term relationships, but needs to be careful not to jump in too young because he might not be ready for commitment until he has experienced more of life. Zac is highly independent and eccentric, but may find it difficult sometimes to express his feelings or discuss problems. His ideal partner is Aries, and her tolerance and understanding would be well rewarded by charm, good taste and loyalty. In a relationship with Zac, there would never be a dull moment.

CHAPTER EIGHT

Write On

What astounds most people about Hanson is the extraordinary depth of their songwriting and the maturity of their lyrics. How can they write about relationships and broken hearts when they haven't experienced these things themselves? No matter. They do, and to be honest it's not important how they do it.

'We've got songs of betrayal and deceit from four years ago,' says Tay defensively. 'The songs are inspired by everyday life. Originally we would write about brothers and sisters. Just whatever we were thinking about. And, of course, girls.'

'We were writing songs about girls long before we even cared,' continues Ike.

Zac, if not his older brothers, still couldn't give a monkey's about the females of the species. But he is the most illuminating about the whole songwriting process. 'When you write a song, it's like you're playing a part in a play. You create the character. You don't have to totally experience it to write about it.'

Hanson's songs are perfectly attuned to the worries and concerns of their fans. Because they write their own music, the songs reflect the feelings and needs of people their own age. 'Even though being a kid is kind of carefree,' says Zac, 'there are definitely a lot of things that stick in kids' minds.'

Ike takes up the thread. 'There's definitely moments of depression in life. But our music focuses on other things instead of being depressed.'

Their upbeat style probably stems from all the sixties' soul that they listened to when they were growing up, as well as their own personalities – you'd be hard-pressed to meet three happier and more optimistic teenagers. But they do listen to modern music too, and that has helped give them an edge to their songwriting.

'We listen to Counting Crows, Aerosmith, the Spin Doctors,' explains Tay. 'We listen to some rap. And since we're from Oklahoma, we listen to some country too.'

Current favourites include No Doubt, Alanis Morrissette, The Cardigans, Billy Joel and Beck.

'There's nobody doing what Beck's doing. It's really unique,' says Tay.

So where is the middle of nowhere? 'Wherever,' says Ike. 'People use the phrase all the time. It was originally a line from "Man From Milwaukee" and, well, we thought that was a cool title, and so here it is.'

The album has a healthy balance of get-up-and-boogie pop anthems, slow rock softies and end-of-the-evening ballads. There's no set way the brothers write their songs and inspiration can come from the least expected of places, but when it does, the floodgates can well and truly open.

'The first song on the album, "Thinking Of You", we were just jamming together, and that song started flowing and in thirty minutes it was written,' says Tay.

If they had all happened that quickly, Hanson could have written the album in a day. It's not always that easy though and the boys never know where their next idea is coming from.

'"Thinking Of You" is a weird example,' says Tay, who must use the word 'weird' more than anyone else on the planet. And, lo and behold, it was the inspiration for another song.

Tay says, 'We were talking about the fact that nobody had ever written a song about "weird". It seemed strange. Think about how many times you say it.' Not the most complex of reasons for writing a hit record, but the end result is a weepy, thoughtful ode to people who are shunned by society because they don't fit in.

The idea for the bonus track on the CD, 'Man From Milwaukee', came to Zac when the family's van broke down – in the middle of nowhere – and they had to wait for their parents to fix it. 'I was sitting at a bus stop when this guy sat down next to me,' he says. 'I'd been thinking about aliens, and I suddenly thought, What if he's really an alien?'

'The point of the song is "don't judge a book by its cover",' says Ike.

'Because at first you think this guy is just nutso, but in the end the man from Milwaukee really is an alien,' adds Tay.

As it turns out, the boys were actually in Albuquerque at the time, on their way to record the album in LA, but Zac changed the song title to the 'Man From Milwaukee' because 'Albuquerque didn't have the right ring to it.'

Elsewhere, you'll find 'Speechless', a melancholy tale about being deceived by your girlfriend; 'Lucy', a heartfelt story of a boy who can't cope after breaking up with a girl he took for granted; 'Yearbook', the mystery of a classmate who disappeared; and perhaps the most achingly poignant track on the album, 'With You In Your Dreams', written for their dying grandma, which has their gran telling them, 'Don't be sad, get on with your lives, remember the good times.'

The boys refuse to pick out a favourite. 'I cannot betray a song. They are too valuable,' says Zac.

Ike is more practical. 'If somebody had just fifteen minutes to listen to the album, I'd say listen to a minute of every song,' he says. 'There's quite a bit of variety – one makes you want to dance, it's really up and makes you feel good, others are just mellow and then some are really intense, it's like, "Wow, now what is this about?"'

Don't even bother asking them to name their favourite song of all time. Zac starts going mental. 'No! I would kill myself,' he says. 'Or I wouldn't kill myself, I would just hit myself. I would go, "Doh, doh, doh, doh"' (punches himself). 'I would go, "I can't do it man, you're asking too much from me."'

CHAPTER NINE

Hanson . . . and
on . . . and on . . .

These days Hanson are greeted by near-deafening screams from hordes of hysterical girls in all four corners of the world. At one concert in Toronto, Canada, the volume of the crowd was recorded at 140 decibels – smashing the previous record of 126 decibels set by a loud sixties' rock group called The Who. The noise of a jet aeroplane taking off is 150 decibels! Not surprisingly, Hanson have to wear earplugs to protect their ears from serious damage while they're on stage.

Apart from Toronto, two recent events really stuck in the Hanson memory. The first was the now-legendary performance at Paramus Park Mall in New Jersey, America, the day after *Middle Of Nowhere* was released. At the last minute a local radio station had organized for

Hanson to play a couple of songs on a temporary stage to plug their single and answer questions afterwards. 'We weren't expecting too much,' says Tay. 'Maybe a couple of hundred people, five hundred at most.'

They were in for the biggest shock of their lives. Even though Hanson weren't supposed to go on stage until 8.30 p.m., excited fans had been turning up since midday. By the time the boys arrived there were 6,000 of them squashed into every conceivable corner. This was Hanson's first taste of fame – and they couldn't quite believe what was happening to them.

Ike says, 'It was, "Ohmigosh – we have a situation."'

Most of the mainly female audience had been waiting for hours and so when Hanson finally appeared they went wild. The boys covered their ears. 'Even then the shrieks would cut through,' says Tay. 'We were just trying to find a way to block out the pain.'

Zac shouted 'Please stop screaming' through the mike, but as soon as Hanson started singing, it began all over again. The boys hadn't brought the equipment with them to cope, thinking it was going to be a low-key appearance. Ike was playing acoustic guitar, Tay had a tambourine and Zac was on maracas. They simply weren't loud enough. The crowd was drowning them out and pushing closer all the time.

'You're not nervous about singing in front of everyone,' said Tay afterwards, 'you're nervous for your life.'

There wasn't enough security to cope and the boys were rushed off after just ten minutes, but not without a few scares. Tay had his shirt ripped as fans reached out to touch him, and Zac, at the back, almost got completely swallowed up by the crowd when he tripped on the stairs. If he had, Hanson might now be a duo!

It wasn't the only time that Hanson have had to run for their lives – and it certainly won't be the last. There was an equally frightening moment on their tour of South-East Asia. In Jakarta, Indonesia, they were scheduled to hold a press conference in the Hard Rock Cafe and then play a three-song acoustic set to journalists and a small number of lucky fans.

But Hanson-mania had already infested the globe and thousands of disappointed fans couldn't get in. When the impatient crowd outside heard Hanson start playing they couldn't control their excitement any longer and pushed past the helpless staff on the door. As more and more girls squeezed inside, the crowd swelled in front of Hanson's eyes. Soon people were almost hanging off the balcony and the press were under siege.

'It turned into a way too big concert,' says Tay. 'The press were going –'

'"What's the deal?"' continues Ike. '"There's kids standing on my shoulders now."'

Halfway through their first song, Hanson were whisked off by their security guard. When some order returned, the boys came back to play their other two songs to a rapturous reception. But things were starting to get out of hand again so, as soon as they'd played their last note, they tried to make their escape. It was just like a James Bond film.

'We got through the kitchen and on to the roof,' recalls Ike. 'We turned around and there were about fifty fans chasing us.'

They tried to sneak through another restaurant to safety, but were spotted again.

'They were grabbing our hair and jumping on us and almost ripping off our clothes,' he says. Eventually they made it back to their van, but even there they were mobbed by crazed girls pounding on the side of the bus and rocking it from side to side.

'It's a bit scary when twenty or thirty people are running at your car,' says Ike.

Meanwhile, the crowd still outside the Hard

Rock began to turn nasty when they heard that Hanson had disappeared. So the bosses decided to let them all in and play a video of the boys' performance. 'Everybody started crying and taking pictures of the screen,' says Zac.

In every country they have visited to promote their album – all over Europe and America and as far away as Taiwan – the boys have had a similar response. In Australia, 20,000 fans turned up to a car park to see them play three acoustic songs, they were mobbed in Japan and brought traffic to a halt in London filming the video for 'Where's The Love'. But Hanson insist that they don't get frightened – much.

'Most fans are not crazy, it's when you get seven thousand of them,' says Tay. 'We've had insane things happen, but the security's more for their sake.'

'So they don't kill each other,' says Zac. 'You wanna keep your fans alive.' Very sensible!

Ike is typically level-headed about their lightning-quick global success. 'Something you realize as you travel around,' he says, 'music is a universal language. When you go to all these different countries and people are singing a song that you wrote – in English – you realize music crosses all boundaries.'

Record label boss, Greenberg, believes the

key to their success is that 'MMMBop's catchy chorus means the same thing in every language. 'Everyone told me kids today would never exhibit hysteria for a young rock band the way they did a generation ago,' he says. 'But kids are kids. They don't change. This reminds me of The Beatles landing at Kennedy Airport.'

This is no throwaway comment – in the 1960s The Beatles were the biggest band the world had ever seen and their fans went wild everywhere they travelled to. Tay can't quite believe the comparison.

'The Beatles! I mean, they were The Beatles. We're ladybug size!'

But times have changed rapidly since the sixties, especially when it comes to technological developments such as television and computers. Today's pop groups are in contact with a global audience and fans have a whole new way to make friends with fellow devotees and to follow their favourite bands' progress, even to watch them playing live on the other side of the world – the Internet.

Hanson are one of the biggest bands in cyber-space. They caused havoc on the Internet during a trip to Europe when an on-line chat session had to be cut short because the computers couldn't cope with the response. Their website (www.hansonline.com) is getting over one million visits per month, making it the most popular music site on the Worldwide Web and they get over 700 e-mails a week. There are over 100 Hanson tribute sites set up and Tay has another fifty sites dedicated just to himself. (Zac has around thirty-five and Ike has thirty.) Plus they get almost 25,000 fan letters a week; 3,000 from the UK. Unlike some pop groups, Hanson take time out to reply to as many as they can, but it's an impossible task. 'We really miss the personal relationship we had with our fans when we were just a friendly little local band,' says Ike. 'It's horrible because we have more fans and less time.'

While they've had an overwhelming response everywhere they've been, the ever-observant teenagers have noticed some peculiarities in the lovestruck crowds.

'Parisian girls are stronger,' says Tay. 'We were at this TV show and there were about fifty girls outside and it was really hard to get through. We went to a mall the other day to do a radio thing and there were about five thousand people there and they were crazy and they were screaming . . .'

'But they weren't pushing as much,' finishes Ike.

'There wasn't as much strength,' continues Tay. 'I mean, there was like some major strength in France. They must have been lifting weights.'

'I think it's part of the culture. It's like that in Latin America too,' concludes Ike.

One thing they don't miss on their travels is their favourite food – you can get burgers, fries and pizzas all over the world. But it doesn't always come how you expect it. They had a shock when they ordered a pizza in France. 'The cheeses they use are like, "Wow",' says Ike.

'As soon as you taste it, it's "I'm awake!"' adds Zac.

And even the toppings weren't right. They ordered their favourite, pepperoni, but Ike says, 'In France, pepperoni means small peppers. And they give you indigestion.'

'Not to mention some major gas,' adds Tay. They are more careful about what they drink, and try to stick to diet versions of their favourite fizzy drinks.

Hanson enjoyed their time in London too, especially Segaworld and the West End musicals, and they took the opportunity to stock up on Doc Martens in every colour imaginable. When they got back to their hotel they could hardly fit them all in the room.

'The nice thing about England is that they actually speak English,' observes Ike.

'England's beautiful,' adds Tay. 'There's just so much more history than there is in the US.'

England was so popular that Hanson moved into a house just outside Reading to record their Christmas album, *Snowed In*.

'We lived there for a whole month and no one knew,' admits Tay. 'We lived in this huge mansion and had our own recording studio right next door.'

The boys found that their English fans were more reserved than their Continental counterparts. 'People think we need a bodyguard,' continues Tay, 'but that's not true. When we lived in England people got used to seeing us and no one hassled us.'

Zac reckons that their favourite place is Australia. 'The beaches just blew us away and there was so much to do,' he says. 'We also like Bali. It was kind of a movie set – all sand and trees.'

As well as visiting some amazing places, they've come across some incredible people too. They met Jon Bon Jovi at a Cardigans concert and Cindy Crawford when they were filming a piece for MTV.

'We met the Spice Girls too,' says Ike. 'They were very nice. And we met Eternal. They are extremely nice ladies.' Cindy Crawford, the Spice Girls, Eternal . . . it's a line-up to make any teenage boy green with envy.

But with success also comes suspicion, despite Hanson being quite possibly the nicest band in the world. Since their rise to fame, rumours, nasty comments and downright lies have been spread by people who are jealous of Hanson's success and find their wholesome image too good to be true. Last year Tay was so furious about evil stories going round Australia that he sent a letter to *Smash Hits*. 'I have not been in a car accident and I am definitely not in a coma,' he wrote. 'I'm not dyslexic either.' He also told people to stop picking on Zac. 'He's not fat. It's just the shape of his body and in a year he'll grow out of it.'

It wasn't much better in their home country, where a nasty rumour was circulating last year saying that Zac was dead. The family were able to laugh it off but it was a very unpleasant story for someone to make up. 'You've just gotta block out those sort of rumours,' says Tay.

Yet another story going round the States says that they don't play their instruments. 'That's a pretty bogus thing to say,' says Ike. Stories like this make you realize that being famous does have its drawbacks.

The boys even get people impersonating them. Some guys pretended to be Hanson during a live phone-in on a radio station in Atlanta, Georgia and started swearing and acting like total idiots. On the Internet, where there are almost as many anti-Hanson sites as there are tribute pages, there have been impostors too. But while many of the websites are openly cruel, others are merely incorrect, some of them amusingly so.

Ike says, 'There's one webpage that says, "Isaac, Taylor and Edgar emigrated from Sweden to the United States to get a record deal. They were originally singing the song, 'Boom-pop', but they changed it to 'MMMBop' after tons of people said it wasn't quite right. Their mother Edith Hanson . . ." And we're going, "Oh my God." We thought about putting a link to it because it was just so outrageously weird.'

Another thing that annoys Hanson is people always calling them girls because of their long blond hair. Ike says, 'I guess people just take a look at the back of our heads and make an assumption.'

'But then we turn round to face them and they go, "Yeeaaarrgh!"' says Zac. 'The only people who say we look like girls are ones who've lost their girlfriends because they like our band,' he adds, putting it in perspective.

'People often think that we grew our hair because of the band, that it's some kind of style thing,' says Tay, 'but we just decided to grow it one day.'

And Ike is perfectly serious when he says, 'We might decide to cut it all off in a week. It doesn't really matter! Hair is hair.'

When a tabloid newspaper asked him whether they would do it for £10,000, he was quite blasé. 'If the right offer came in, of course I'd cut my hair. Ten thousand pounds seems about right to me. It's not a big deal. We cut it quite often anyway.'

Oh, and one last thing, they're tired of everyone asking if they use any special secret ingredient to keep it so shiny and bouncy. They don't. 'Just shampoo and conditioner,' says Ike.

Amidst all this commotion, it's incredible that these three excitable and hyperactive brothers have not gone off the rails. They may sometimes get impatient on their travels (they once made themselves extremely unpopular with all the rich guests at a five-star hotel for rollerblading across the third floor), but then boys will be boys after all. Despite the accolades, they are still the same sweet brothers that everyone liked when they were growing up in Tulsa. They still go rollerblading and hang out in the shopping mall, although the last time they went they got kicked out of a toy shop for bouncing balls around.

'Success isn't important in our eyes. All that really matters is making music,' states Zac.

'We never said we wanted to be rock stars,' adds Tay. 'But I guess if you play music and people like it, you become rock stars. People may not believe us but we're not doing this because we want girls to scream, and to make lots of money – we're doing this because we love music. But girls can scream if they want. We could get used to it. Hey, we could even learn to love it.'

They're going to have to.

CHAPTER TEN

The Future

In just one short year Hanson have sprung from the middle of nowhere to become the princes of pop. Now, they have the world at their feet. Their music has made them millionaires, they are adored everywhere from Skegness to South-East Asia and they have been showered with offers from TV companies and Hollywood bosses.

Hanson's spokesperson has already denied claims that the boys have been involved in talks to star in their own real-life sitcom, loosely based on the cult sixties' TV programme *The Monkees* (which starred a pop group of the same name). However, a Christmas TV special featuring the brothers called *Meet Hanson* went down a storm and only served to fuel rumours of further small screen work. After the success of the Spice Girls' movie, actors' magazine *Variety* and some newspapers reported last year that Hanson had already sold their story to an independent film company, but the boys don't know anything about it.

However, they don't rule out the possibility of a celluloid career. 'We're open to anything – eventually we could act,' says Zac.

'We've done videos for other people a long time ago and we love all that,' adds Tay.

But for the time being, Hanson don't want to spread their interests too wide.

'We get lots of offers,' says Zac, 'but what we want to focus on is our music. We have at least two hundred more songs.' Hanson are so prolific, they are even keen to write songs for other people.

Yet their biggest buzz comes not from the studio but from playing live. 'Seeing all those kids just come to see you play,' says Ike, 'that's a pretty great feeling. It's just so cool that all these people are having fun and dancing or clapping to your music.'

Their concerts are sold out the world over, but the boys insist that they would still make music if no one turned up.

'Even if the fans hated our music we couldn't stop,' says Tay.

But though Hanson are riding on the crest of a wave right now, will they be able to cope with the pressures of fame in years to come?

Pete Waterman, the man who launched the pop careers of former *Neighbours* stars Kylie Minogue and Jason Donovan, warns, 'Hanson will need daily schooling and they'll find touring really difficult. At first, it's fun and sexy, but it takes its toll. Fame changes your lifestyle and I don't believe you can balance that because the public are insatiable. They want Hanson now.'

However, Ike insists that Hanson will be around for a long time to come.

'We're not going to crack up,' he says. 'We have a really great relationship with each other, with our parents, with our brothers and sisters, really good friends, and that's something that keeps you grounded, that keeps you from that kind of pressure.'

Zac is ready for the worst though. When asked what he wanted to be doing in the next millennium he said, 'I wanna be a worker at Burger King.'

One thing that will stand Hanson in good stead is the quality of their songwriting – a cut above most of the teen bands that have gone before them and indeed many of the far older groups that are around the charts at the moment. The Hanson motto has always been: 'Judge us by our music not our age' and the boys are mature enough to take whatever the future holds in their stride.

'We're just going to be ourselves,' says Ike, 'and we're going to cross our fingers and hope that people like it. Because that's all you can do.'

Tay adds, 'If we get to do this for the rest of our lives, to make a living off something that we really do love, instead of some nine to five . . . that would be awesome.'

The boys also realize that if Hanson hadn't come along, another band would probably have taken their place. 'If you're not there, somebody else is going to be. So be happy while you are because it can be gone,' says Ike. 'You have to remember that this kind of thing can go just as fast as it can come – and it's come really fast, so it can go just as fast.'

It's clear that Hanson intend to make the most of their success while they can.

'Being successful's like having a birthday,' says Tay. 'It's amazing.'

But doesn't it annoy them that they can't leave the house without being mobbed?

'Sure, it may not be fun at times,' agrees Tay. 'But if cameras follow you around everywhere, the minute that ends, you'll wish it was there.'

For now, Hanson are going to enjoy the high life – well, as high as you can get by their standards. Despite having more money in the bank than most people could even dream about, they are extremely reluctant to spend it.

'We may get a big house or a slightly nicer car,' says Ike.

Tay is even more sensible. 'We'll just invest it in doing more music. We're going to build a studio at home, which'll save us money in the future and make our next record better than the last one.'

The only luxury they might allow themselves is improving their Lego collection.

Tay says, 'We'll get more Lego whether we're visionaries –'

'Or whether we're zeronaries,' finishes Ike.

The biggest threat to Hanson is the onset of puberty. Tay's voice is already breaking and Zac's will follow in a couple of years. The question is whether they will still sound as good afterwards. Even that doesn't faze them. 'We could sing in high voices like the Bee Gees,' jokes Ike.

Hanson are such good musicians, so devoted to each other and so pumped full of self-belief that they will keep going no matter what. They are one of the biggest bands on the planet and if there are any music-loving aliens out there, Hanson will probably win them over too.

One thing's certain, the next year promises to be as crazy as the last. And no doubt, the year after that and the year after that . . . Because Ike has great news for all Hanson fans: 'Music is a part of us and it's what we've always done. We intend to be doing it for a long time. And if we weren't doing music, then we wouldn't be who we are, because music is our life. That's what we love. We'll be doing this for another twenty-five years.'